EGYPT

A TRUE BOOK

by

Elaine Landau

Children's Press®

A Division of Grolier Publishing

New York London Hong Kong Sydney
Danbury, Connecticut

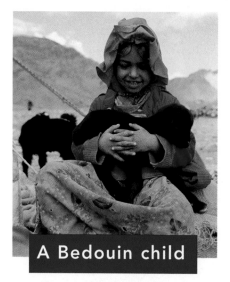

A Bedouin child

Reading Consultant
Linda Cornwell
*Coordinator of School Quality
and Professional Improvement
Indiana State Teachers
Association*

Author's Dedication
For Michael

**Visit Children's Press® on the
Internet at:
http://publishing.grolier.com**

Library of Congress Cataloging-in-Publication Data

Egypt / by Elaine Landau.
    p.   cm.—(A true book)
Includes bibliographical references and index.
Summary: Discusses the history, geography, people, government, and economy of Egypt.
   ISBN: 0-516-21172-2 (lib. bdg.)   0-516-27018-4 (pbk.)
   1. Egypt—Juvenile literature. [1. Egypt.] I. Title. II. Series
DT49.L296 2000
962—dc21
                                 99-25975
                                       CIP
                                       AC

GROLIER
PUBLISHING

Contents

A mummy is a prized part of a museum's Egyptian collection.

Ancient and Modern

Picture pyramids, temple ruins, and mummies. Where could you find all of these? If you said ancient Egypt—you're right.

Egypt is in the northeastern corner of Africa. It is a rectangular-shaped land bordered by the Mediterranean Sea to the north, Sudan to the south, and

Libya to the west. Israel and the Red Sea lie to the east. A small part of Egypt called the Sinai Peninsula lies in Asia.

The weather in Egypt is fairly warm and dry. Autumn and winter temperatures are usually between 60 and 80 degrees Fahrenheit (15 and 27 degrees Celsius). During the summer, temperatures may rise to over 114 degrees F (46 C). The Mediterranean coast gets about 8 inches (20

These ships were the first to sail through the Suez Canal at opening ceremonies in 1869.

the Suez Canal to the British government. The Suez Canal, built years earlier by a French company, linked the Mediterranean Sea and the Red Sea, greatly reducing the sailing distance from Europe to east Asia. Britain wanted full control of the Suez Canal, and in 1882 it invaded Egypt.

Under British control, the royal dynasty established by Muhammad Ali reigned in name only. Although the British made some important improvements in Egypt, the Egyptian people bitterly resented their presence. In 1922, Britain finally granted Egypt its independence.

King Farouk I (left); President Nasser at a conference in Cairo, 1956 (right)

Egypt's royal dynasty ended in 1952 when Egyptian army officers, led by Gamal Abdel Nasser, forced King Farouk I, Muhammad Ali's last ruling descendant, to leave the throne. In 1953, Egypt became a republic.

A Wonderful

This diver examines a sphinx.

Dozens of ancient artifacts lie underwater in the harbor of Alexandria. Divers have found the remains of one of the ancient Seven Wonders of the World—the Lighthouse of Alexandria. Greek king Ptolemy II built it in the 200s B.C.

The Lighthouse of Alexandria

Discovery

A large mirror and a fire provided the light to guide ships through dangerous, rocky waters. The lighthouse stood for about 1,500 years before powerful earthquakes weakened its structure, and it finally tumbled into the sea. Today, Egyptian authorities plan to build a museum to display some of the sphinxes and statues recovered.

A statue is brought to the surface.

The People

Although Egypt has a land area of 385,229 square miles (997,739 sq. km), most Egyptians live near the Nile River or the Suez Canal. Within this fertile region, almost half of the people live in cities while the rest live in some four thousand villages in the deserts and mountains.

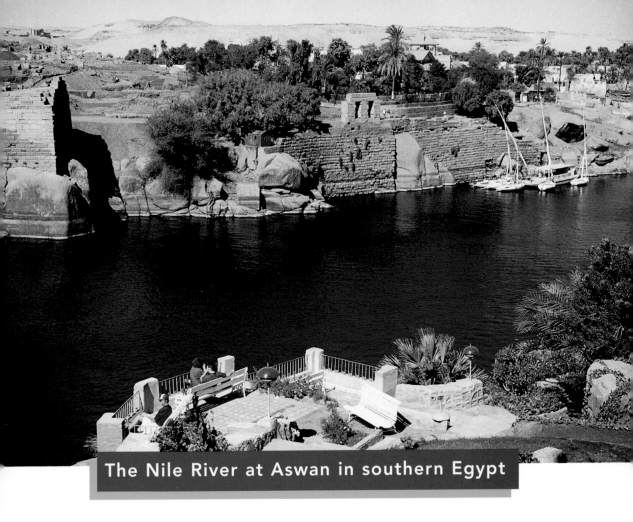

The Nile River at Aswan in southern Egypt

Religion plays an important role in Egypt. Most Egyptians are Sunni Muslims. A devout Muslim prays five times a day

Bowing toward the holy city of Mecca, a man stops to pray.

and follows Islamic laws. Minority religious groups include Egyptian Copts, a Christian group who make up a small part of the population and an even smaller number of Jews.

The Bedouin are nomads who wander in the desert with

their animals. In recent times, many Bedouin have settled down and become farmers. Nubians, from the south of Egypt, are the largest non-Arab group. There are also some Italians and Greeks in Egypt.

These Bedouin men (left) are drinking breakfast tea. This Nubian girl (right) lives in southern Egypt.

A view of Cairo and the Citadel, a restored 12th-century fortress (above); A mosque in downtown Alexandria (right)

Life in Egypt's cities differs sharply from village life. Cairo, Egypt's capital, is the largest city in Africa. Cairo and Alexandria, Egypt's second-largest city, face many of the problems seen in urban regions throughout the world today. Widespread overcrowding results in makeshift housing and a lack of public transportation and community services. Great wealth and dreadful poverty exist in Egypt's cities.

Egyptians are drawn to the cities for a better life.

Home can be a charming waterfront apartment (left) or a corner in a slum district (right).

Beautiful homes are found near slums. Well-educated Egyptians are employed in various professions and businesses. People without skills often work as laborers.

More than half of all Egypt's people live in the countryside. These are mostly farmers or peasants who rent small plots of land. Most of them live in mud brick homes with straw roofs.

Unfortunately, only half of adult Egyptians can read and write. Boys are more likely to be educated than girls, so twice as many Egyptian men as women can read. Many students go to high school. Few of them, however, go on to college. Some students attend one of Egypt's thirteen universities and some go to school in other countries. All of Egypt's schools are government controlled and free, including universities.

People who live and work in cities usually dress like people in North America and Europe.

Wearing traditional robes, this man holds the key to an ancient tomb.

In Egypt, Muslim women cover their bodies (left) for practical as well as religious reasons. For her wedding, this woman wears a decorative covering called a *burkua* (right).

Poor people in both cities and villages tend to wear more traditional Egyptian clothing.

In recent years, more Egyptian women have dressed according to Islamic teachings. They wear long robes and a veil that covers their arms, ears, and hair.

Egyptian food includes a great variety of fruits, vegetables, and fish. For breakfast, most Egyptians have *ful medames*—cooked dried beans mashed into a paste with olive oil and spices. It is eaten by dipping bread into the paste. Lamb or mutton is the most

Fresh baked bread (left) and fried meat cakes (right)

popular meat. It is often served on kabobs—cut in chunks and cooked on a skewer with onions and peppers. Grape leaves stuffed with rice are popular as well.

Soccer is a favorite sport in Egypt, and many people enjoy handball, squash, and tennis.

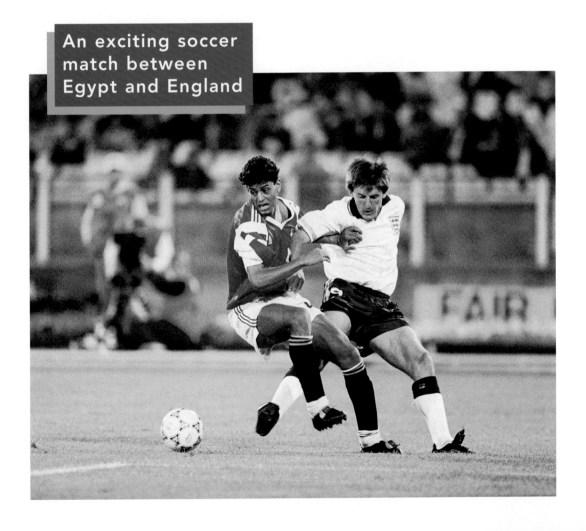

An exciting soccer match between Egypt and England

This group enjoys a drink at an outdoor cafe.

But recreation usually means socializing with friends. Egyptians like to sit and talk with one another while sipping thick, sweet coffee flavored with spices. They also enjoy sweet tea.

Economy

Egypt faces difficulties in industry and business today. Industrial growth has not kept up with the growing population. There are problems in agriculture, as well. In the past, the nation produced enough food for its people. But now nearly

Workers on an Egyptian oil rig

half its food has to be imported.

Egypt exports petroleum, raw cotton, cement, rubber products, and other manufactured goods. However, earnings from exports do not meet the cost of the nation's imports. And funds from tourism and the Suez Canal do not close this gap. As a result, Egypt has had to borrow money from other countries.

Government

Egypt's constitution, adopted in 1971, calls its government an "Arab Republic." It has three branches—an executive branch, a legislative branch known as the People's Assembly, and a judicial branch, or court system.

An Egyptian president may serve an unlimited number of

six-year terms. The president appoints one or more vice presidents as well as his Council of Ministers, or cabinet. As in the United States, the Egyptian president heads the nation's armed forces.

Like the U.S. Supreme Court, Egypt's Supreme Constitutional Court determines whether laws are constitutional. The nation's legal system is based on Islamic, English, and French law.

Present Day

As an Arab nation, Egypt has been involved in wars with Israel in 1947, 1956, 1967, and 1973. In 1978, however, Egyptian President Anwar el-Sadat took a bold step to end the conflict. He met with Israeli Prime Minister Menachem Begin and U.S. President Jimmy Carter to work out a peace plan.

At the Camp David Accords (from left): Egyptian President Sadat, U.S. President Carter, and Israeli Prime Minister Begin

The result—the Camp David Accords—led to the first peace treaty between an Arab nation and Israel.

Unfortunately, other Arab nations condemned Sadat and rejected the peace treaty he signed in 1979. Islamic extremists caused unrest in the region. In

October 1981, Sadat was assassinated by members of his own army who believed he had betrayed his country.

Hosni Mubarak, the next Egyptian president, kept the peace with Israel and maintained relations with the United States. Mubarak has also tried to mend Egypt's ties with other Arab states.

President Mubarak speaks at a summit meeting with other Arab leaders.

Young Egyptians attend a rally.

By the 1990s, Egypt also had to deal with terrorist attacks by Islamic extremists. They wanted to hurt Egypt's economy by discouraging tourists and foreign investors.

The Egyptian government is actively working to improve education and industry as well as to fight terrorism. Many feel certain that a country with such a splendid past will surely have a brighter future.

To Find Out More

Here are some additional resources to help you learn more about the nation of Egypt:

 **Books**

Clayton, Peter A. **The Valley of the Kings.** Thomson Learning, 1995.

Der Manuelian, Peter. **Hieroglyphs from A to Z.** Scholastic, 1996.

Harvey, Miles. **Look What Came from Egypt.** Franklin Watts, 1998.

James, John and Louise. **How We Know about the Egyptians.** Peter Bedrick Books, 1997.

Morley, Jacqueline. **How Would You Survive As an Ancient Egyptian?** Franklin Watts, 1996.

Wilcox, Charlotte. **Mummies and Their Mysteries.** Carolrhoda, 1993.

Organizations and Online Sites

**Egypt State
Information Service**
http://www.us.sis.gov.eg/

Includes images from Egypt's major historical periods, plus the latest information on topics such as politics, culture, and economy.

**Egyptian Galleries@the
University of Pennsylvania
Museum of Archaeology
and Anthropology**
*http://www.upenn.edu/
museum/Collections/
egyptianframedoc1.html*

Write and print out your name in hieroglyphs, visit the Egyptian galleries, and learn all about human and animal mummification. Click on the magic dice for "Fun and Games."

Little Horus Web Site
http://www.horus.ics.org.eg/

Learn about Egypt today as well as its ancient history, join a club, and read a letter from Egypt's first lady, Mrs. Suzanne Mubarak.

Odyssey Online: Egypt
*http://www.emory.edu/
CARLOS/ODYSSEY/EGYPT/
homepg.html*

Follow the trotting camel to find out about people, mythology, daily life, death and burial, and more. Meet your guide, Rosetta Stone, then play an amulet matching game.

Tour Egypt
http://touregypt.net/

The official site of Egypt's Ministry of Tourism also features fun stuff. Take an online safari, explore The Pharaonic Village, and check out the interactive recipe book.

Important Words

descendant the offspring of a particular person or group of people

devout devoted to religion

extremist someone who uses radical methods to bring about change

hieroglyphics a form of picture writing developed by the ancient Egyptians

Muslim a follower of the faith of Islam

pharaoh a ruler in ancient Egypt

republic a nation in which the people vote for their governing officials

territorial having to do with a specific area of land or territory

treaty a formal agreement between two or more nations

urban concerning cities

Index

Meet the Author

Elaine Landau worked as a newspaper reporter, an editor, and a youth services librarian before becoming a full-time writer. She has written more than one hundred nonfiction books for young people, including True Books on dinosaurs, animals, countries, and food.

Ms. Landau, who has a bachelor's degree in English and journalism from New York University and a master's degree in library and information science from Pratt Institute, lives in Florida with her husband and son.